PIONEERS OF SCIENCE

KU-260-732

MARIE CURIE

Andrew Dunn

Pioneers of Science

Archimedes

Alexander Graham Bell

Karl Benz

Marie Curie

Michael Faraday

Leonardo da Vinci

Guglielmo Marconi

Isaac Newton

Series editor Rosemary Ashley
Designer David Armitage

First published in 1990 by
Wayland (Publishers) Limited
61 Western Road, Hove
East Sussex BN3 1JD, England

© 1990 Wayland (Publishers) Limited

British Library Cataloguing in Publication Data
Dunn, Andrew
  Marie Curie.
  1. Chemistry. Curie Marie
  I. Title II. Series
  540.92

  ISBN 1–85210–955–6

Typeset by Nicola Taylor, Wayland.
Printed in Italy by Rotolito Lombarda S.p.A.
Bound in France by A.G.M.

Contents

1 Introduction

As we approach the end of the twentieth century, we can see around us a world full of scientific wonders. This story is about a discovery that made many of those things possible. It is the story of quiet, shy Marie Curie, the brilliant scientist who found radium for us.

Radium gives off penetrating rays. Marie Curie called this powerful effect 'radioactivity', and began to investigate it. Her discovery also gave other scientists the clues they needed to find out what atoms are. They began to look into the mysteries of the tiny atom and to understand this building block, from which everything in the universe is made.

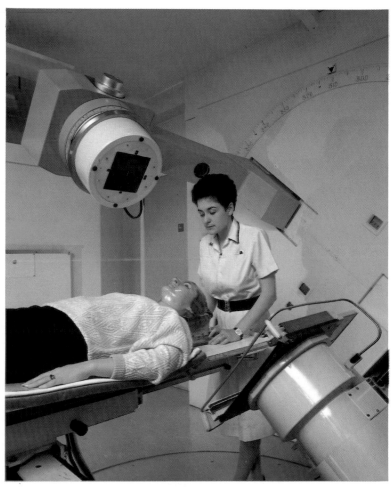

A patient with cancer being prepared for treatment by radiation, one of today's uses of Marie Curie's discoveries.

Radioactivity is used in many different ways. In medicine, it helps to diagnose and then treat diseases, especially cancer, which used to be incurable. Now, with the help of radioactivity, some forms of cancer can be cured completely. Radioactivity is also used widely in industry: to check products in factories, to find cracks in metal or concrete, to trace pollution, and to find problems in places where people cannot go – such as inside pipelines or deep under the sea.

Nuclear reactors, using radioactive materials as fuel, make huge amounts of electricity all around the world. Nuclear power allows submarines to stay underwater for years at a time. It also powers spacecraft that travel to the very edge of the solar system, sending back pictures from thousands of millions of kilometres away. It may soon drive our cars too.

A modern nuclear reactor at Dounreay in Scotland.

Sadly, Marie Curie's discovery, and the knowledge of the atom, later gave birth to the frightening nuclear weapons that have given humans the power to destroy their planet. We now know how *dangerous* radio-activity is as well. If it is not handled with great care, it can cause cancer and other diseases, and harm unborn babies.

A 'button' of uranium. Uranium is the radioactive fuel used inside nuclear reactors and as an explosive in nuclear weapons.

6

A hundred years ago, not even the most imaginative writer of science fiction could have dreamed of such things. At that time, scientists thought that the atom was the smallest thing there was. They had no idea that the atom has a tiny nucleus at its core, with charged particles called electrons swarming around it. They had no idea that locked up in the atom were fabulous amounts of energy – energy that could be harnessed, for good or ill.

Something else was different then, too. Now, many scientists, doctors and engineers are women. Just a century ago there were almost none.

Scientists at work in the laboratory of a modern Marie Curie Research Institute.

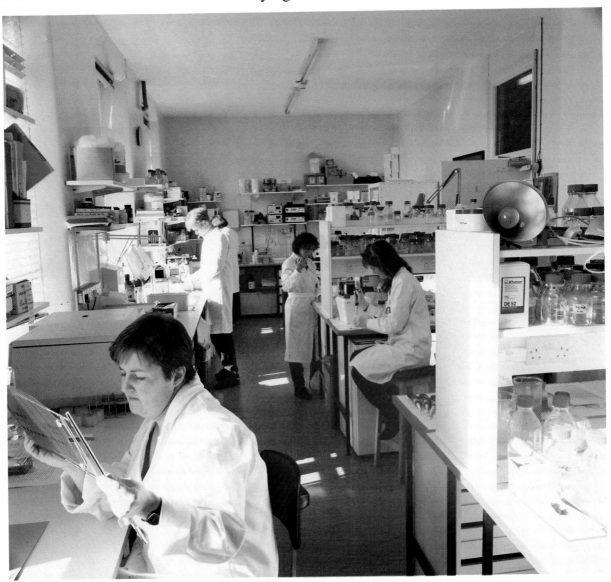

Marie Curie did more than any other person to bring about these changes. Together with her husband Pierre, she discovered radium, one of the most radioactive elements known. She realized that atoms must have an internal structure. She was the first woman to become a professor of science, or to win a Nobel prize (in fact she won *two*). She was the most famous woman of science who has ever lived. Yet she refused to let her discoveries make her rich, because that might prevent others benefiting from them. She did her most important work in appalling conditions. In the end, she gave her life for science.

Marie Curie's name lives on in Cancer Care Homes like this one in England.

2 Manya

Although Marie Curie lived most of her life in France, she was born in November 1867 in Warsaw, the capital of Poland. Her name then was Marya Sklodowska. Her mother was principal of a school, in the old quarter of Warsaw, and her father taught science in another school nearby. Soon after Marya was born, he found a better job as a professor and under-inspector at the high school. The family moved there, and Marya's mother gave up her job to look after her young children.

Marya was the baby of the family. The eldest, Zosia, was six. Then came Jozef, four, and two more sisters, Bronya and Hela. Those were the names they used for each other, and from Marya's very earliest days, they called her Manya.

A street scene in Warsaw, in the early part of the twentieth century. Marya grew up in Poland's capital city.

9

The Sklodowskis were a big, noisy, happy family, very close, warm, and loving, but the life they led was far from easy. When Manya was born Poland was ruled

by the Russian Tsar. The Russians had crushed a rebellion there only four years earlier and were determined to make sure the people did not rebel again. So they began to remove all the Poles from important jobs, and forbade teachers to use the Polish language, or to teach their pupils about Poland's history, traditions or folklore. As a result, when Manya was six, the family came back from their summer holiday to find a letter saying that Manya's father was no longer an under-inspector. His salary was reduced, and he would have to live somewhere else.

The family moved to a new apartment and, because they had less money than before, they had to take in boarders from the school to make ends meet. Soon the house was so crowded that Manya had to sleep on the sofa in the drawing-room. She had to get up at dawn so that the family could eat breakfast.

Then one day, tragedy came to the family. Bronya and Zosia caught a fever. Doctors said it was typhoid, and there was nothing they could do but wait and hope. For days, the two girls burned with the fever. Gradually, Bronya began to recover. But Zosia grew worse. The other children saw her for one last time before she died. Manya, only eight years old, was very sad.

There was another reason for the family to worry. Ever since Manya was born, her mother had been ill. She cared a lot for her family, and cooked, and mended, and made dresses and shoes for her children. Manya could not understand why her adoring mother never hugged or kissed her – she would only stroke her curly hair and send her to play with a friendly pat. The reason was that Manya's mother had tuberculosis – a disease of the lungs which was common in those days. When Zosia died, her mother was too ill to go to the funeral. Manya and her two remaining sisters often went to church to pray for her. When Manya was ten, her mother died, and this affected her for many years. It also made her wonder about the goodness of God, and later in her life she lost all faith in religion.

Opposite This Russian Church in Warsaw is an indication of the strong influence Poland's Russian rulers had on the culture of the country.

Although the family never had enough money, Manya's parents made sure the children had a love of learning. Her father spoke Russian, French, German and English as well as Polish. He had many books at home and would often read to his children in the evenings. He had a collection of instruments, of bright glass and burnished brass, some rocks, even an instrument with gold leaf in it. When she was very young, Manya asked him what they were. 'Physics apparatus,' he replied. Manya always remembered this.

All the children were clever, but the family realized quite early that Manya was especially brilliant. She learned to read before her elder sister Bronya, and after that liked nothing better than to bury her nose in books. One evening, Manya was reading at the table with her hands firmly over her ears to shut out the hubbub. Carefully her sisters and brother piled a tower of chairs around and over her. While they stifled their giggles, Manya noticed nothing... until at last she raised her head – and the furniture came crashing down. She did not see the joke. 'That's stupid!' she said, and left the room.

At school Manya was always top of her class. She learned quickly, and read everything she could, particularly about science. When she finished school at the age of fifteen, she was awarded a gold medal. Manya was the best pupil of her year in the whole of Warsaw, as Jozef and Bronya had been before her. Her father was proud of her and her hard work, but he thought she had perhaps been working too hard. He decided she should have a year off, in the country, staying with relatives.

For a whole year, Manya did no studying. She learned to ride a horse. She read novels, walked in woods and played games with her cousins; she went fishing for shrimps by night, and found a lifelong love for the countryside. And in winter, up in the snowy mountains of Carpathia, she went by sleigh to party after party, and danced until dawn.

A view of the Carpathian Mountains in about 1895, where the young Marie Sklodowska enjoyed a carefree time before she began to devote her life to science.

13

3 Teacher and Student

All too soon Manya's carefree year was over and she had to face the future. Hela wanted to be a singer, but the other three children wanted to study. Jozef was already at the university in Warsaw, learning to be a doctor. Manya wanted desperately to go there too, to study science. Her sister Bronya wanted to be a doctor like Jozef. But Polish universities did not accept girls. If they wanted to study, they had to go abroad, to Paris perhaps, where the famous Sorbonne University admitted female students. The family could never afford that. Unless Bronya and Manya could save enough money themselves, university education was simply out of the question.

A scientist working in one of the Marie Curie Cancer Research Institutes.

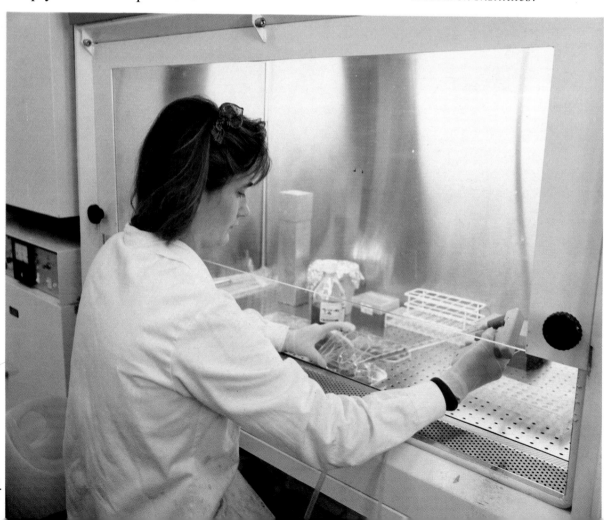

So they began giving private lessons in people's homes, but found it difficult to earn enough to live, let alone save anything. Paris seemed more and more like an impossible dream, out of reach. But they could study in Warsaw, secretly. They joined a group of young people in what they called 'The Floating University', meeting in private rooms all over Warsaw in the evenings, with someone keeping a look-out for the secret police. They talked of the new ideas in philosophy, politics and – most interesting of all to Manya – science. The young people of Poland wanted to be ready for the day when the Russian rulers were overthrown.

Manya realized that she and Bronya could never make enough money to get to Paris like this. But what if they went one at a time? If Manya worked as a governess, she could support Bronya in Paris. Then, when Bronya qualified as a doctor, she could support Manya while she studied science.

Soon Bronya was off to Paris, and Manya found a job as a governess, living with a Warsaw family, helping with the children's education. Unfortunately, the parents were unpleasant and mean. Manya wrote to a friend, 'I shouldn't like my worst enemy to live in such a hell.' She quickly found another job, out in the country, where there were no tempting shops in which to spend what little money she had.

Charles Darwin the English naturalist, whose theories of evolution were among the scientific ideas discussed at Marie's 'Floating University' in Warsaw.

The Sorbonne University in Paris. The Sorbonne was one of the first universities to admit women to scientific studies.

For three years she endured a lonely life. She felt trapped and cut off. She tried to learn what little she could from the few books she had, but it seemed so inadequate, such a waste of time. Sometimes Manya felt that she would never get to Paris and never be a scientist. Then, in the spring of 1890, a letter came from Bronya. She was engaged to another student doctor. He would qualify in a year's time, and then they would marry. So next year Manya could come and live with them and begin her studies at the Sorbonne.

It was a big step. Luggage, even her bed, was sent ahead, and Manya prepared provisions for the three-day journey. When the train left the station, Manya felt nothing but happiness. She was twenty-three, and her life was about to begin again.

Bronya and her husband had many Polish friends in Paris and their flat was often full of music and laughter. But Manya had come to Paris to learn. She signed on for her course with great excitement – with her new French name, Mademoiselle *Marie* Sklodowska.

She soon realized she was going to have to work very hard. Bronya's flat was too full of distraction, so Marie found herself a cheap attic room, nearer the university.

Opposite Pierre Curie, the brilliant physicist, who was introduced to Marie in 1894.

16

Above Paris at the end of the nineteenth century.

There she did nothing but study and sleep. She often forgot to eat. After the day's lectures were over, she read in the library, which was warm. When the library closed for the evening, she worked on in her tiny cold room, often into the small hours of the night.

She was very careful with her tiny supply of money, but it still trickled away. Sometimes she had to choose between food and warmth. She could not afford both, so she was often ill with exhaustion and hunger. But her single-minded determination paid dividends. She sat for her master's degree in physics in the summer of 1893. When the results were announced, she could not believe her ears. She was first in the class! The next year she took another degree, in mathematics.

Early in 1894, Marie met Pierre Curie. She had been asked by the French Society for the Encouragement of National Industry to do some research into magnetism in steel. It was exciting – her first paid scientific job – but she needed somewhere to work. A friend suggested Pierre might help, and introduced them.

Pierre was a tall, thoughtful, quiet man, about nine years older than Marie, and already well-known as a brilliant physicist. He liked this intelligent young woman, and he offered her space in his laboratory. Soon they had fallen in love, and in July 1895 they married. Marie Sklodowska became Marie Curie. They celebrated by taking their new bicycles – wedding presents from Poland – on honeymoon in the green and sunny countryside of France.

They were very happy. Marie was still working on her steel project, but she learned how to cook and keep house too. On the way to the laboratory, she would stop at the vegetable market; on the way home, she would pick up a loaf and some milk. After supper, the couple would sit at either end of their only table, working quietly.

In 1896 Marie took another examination to qualify her to teach – and came top of the list again. There was another cycling tour that summer, then, in 1897, she discovered that she was pregnant. It made life more difficult, but she still carried on with her work. On 12 September, 1897, their first daughter, Irène, was born.

Marie and Pierre with Irène, their eldest daughter. She, too, grew up to become a famous scientist.

4 Radium

When Marie finished the steel project, she had no doubt about what to do next. She would study to become a Doctor of Science just as Pierre had done. To become a Doctor of Science, a student needs to explore some aspect of science that nobody else has examined. So Marie began to look for a field of science that she could investigate.

In late 1897 scientists around the world were already investigating the newly-discovered X-rays. So instead, Marie chose to explore something that seemed, at first, less exciting.

Wilhelm Röntgen, the discoverer of X-rays, at work in his laboratory.

X-rays

The end of the nineteenth century was a very exciting time for science. Two years earlier, many scientists thought they knew almost all there was to know about physics. But on 8 November, 1895, a German physicist called Wilhelm Röntgen noticed something that would change the course of science. By pure chance he discovered that some equipment he was using produced rays which went through solid matter. In fact they went through the wall into the next room. He did not know what they were, so he called them 'X'-rays, 'X' for mystery.

X-rays astounded the world. In a public demonstration in January 1896, Röntgen used them to make a photograph of the bones inside a friend's hand. Doctors saw its potential – for 'seeing' a bullet in a soldier's leg, for example – straight away. The picture below is the first X-ray image. Röntgen made the picture of his wife's hand and the ring she was wearing.

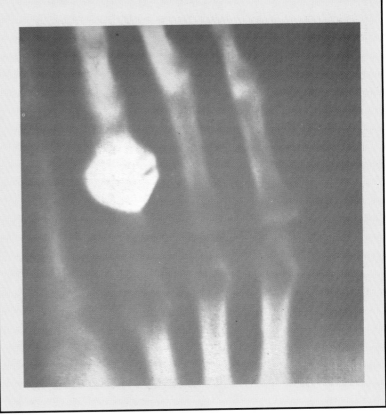

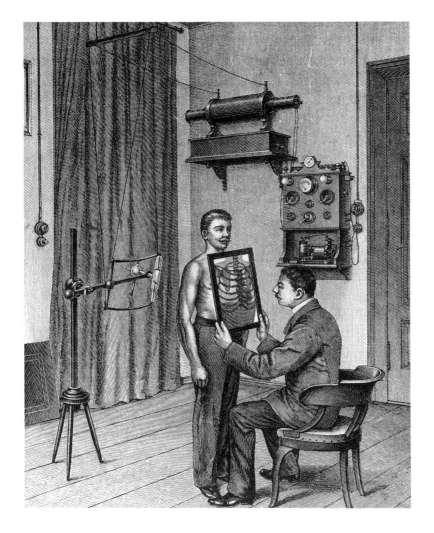

A doctor examining a patient's chest using an X-ray tube (behind the patient) and a fluorescent screen to see the picture of the bones. Now that we know how dangerous radiation is, X-ray machines focus the rays much more carefully (see the illustration on page 40).

Two months after X-rays had been discovered, a French scientist called Henri Becquerel found – again, by pure chance – that very similar rays were given off by a metal called uranium. His rays also passed through solid matter, even through a sheet of aluminium. He called his discovery the 'uranic rays'.

Here was some completely uncharted, unexplored territory. Marie Curie decided to explore *this* mystery herself. But where could she work? She had no laboratory. Eventually she was given a small store-room in the department where Pierre worked. It was damp, it had hardly any furniture, no proper electricity supply, and it was very cold. But it would have to do. So there, in her usual methodical way, Marie Curie began her research.

The Elements

Uranium is a chemical element. Hydrogen, oxygen, carbon, copper, iron, gold and silver, are all elements, each made of its own kind of atom. Everything else is made from combinations, or compounds, of the elements – air, water, wood, stone, the food we eat, even our bodies. In 1898, scientists knew of eighty-three elements. Hydrogen was the lightest, and the heaviest was uranium.

Marie and Pierre photographed in their laboratory while they were making their experiments in the radioactivity of radium in 1898.

Marie began by carefully testing every known element. Within a few days, she had found that one other element also gave off rays – a rare metal called thorium. She could no longer use the term 'uranic rays'. Marie began to call the effect 'radioactivity'.

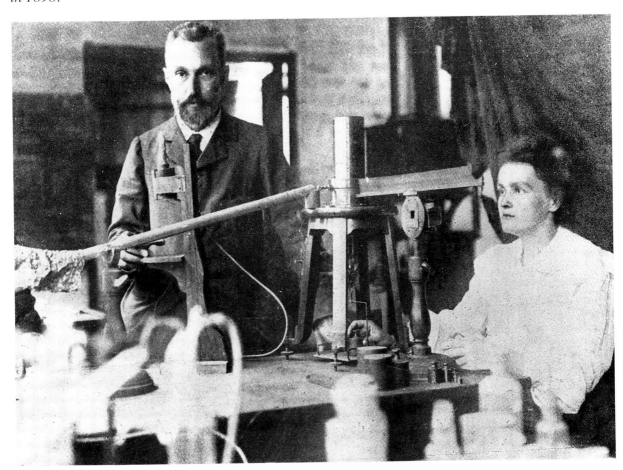

She also discovered that it did not matter whether the material was wet or dry, powdered or lumpy, or what it was mixed with. The amount of radioactivity depended only on the amount of the material. So it could not be a chemical reaction, or a reaction between different atoms, that was making the rays.

It took her a while to realize what this meant: it could only be something *inside* the atom itself. Atoms were not small solid balls after all, as people thought. There must be even smaller particles inside them. Looking back now, we can see that this was the most important discovery she ever made.

Meanwhile there was more work to do. Marie began to study all the minerals containing uranium that she could beg or borrow from friends. Soon she came across a puzzling uranium mineral ore called pitchblende. It was much more radioactive than pure uranium. That could only mean that pitchblende contained something that was far more active than uranium. Chemists had already analyzed pitchblende, and yet they had missed this. So whatever it was could be present only in tiny amounts, but its energy had to be enormous. What could it be? Marie had already tested every known element. With a thrill of excitement, she realized she had discovered a completely *unknown* element. She decided she would call it 'polonium', after her beloved country, to preserve a name which the Russians had officially removed from the map.

For a young scientist, this was a triumphant beginning. But in science, a fact is not a fact until it has been proved. Marie knew that to convince other scientists, she would have to show them her new element. It was in there somewhere, and somehow she would have to extract it. Pierre was by now so curious that he decided to join Marie in her work. In the middle of April 1898, with great excitement, they began – with one hundred grammes of pitchblende, and a pestle and mortar to grind it with.

It was to take four long, exhausting years. It was a very difficult time for both of them. They often felt tired. They had little money and lived very simply. Their entire lives were spent in the small cold laboratory. It was boring, repetitive and physically hard work. Marie's powerful and persistent character, her determination and her hunger for knowledge kept them going. Her method was simple. She would remove all the known elements from the ore by grinding it and dissolving it in acid. Then whatever was left must be the new element. The pitchblende they started with was four times as active as uranium. Each time they removed more of the other elements, what was left was always more active than before. By June they had made a sample that was three hundred times as active as uranium.

Marie and Pierre's work was to make them famous all over the world. This picture appeared on the cover of a French magazine in 1904.

25

By July, they had confirmed that polonium existed. But they soon realized that there was another, even more radioactive element in the ore. Marie called it radium. It was destined to become far, far more famous than polonium, and it would make the name Marie Curie known all around the world.

The wooden shed which became the Curies' laboratory, and where they finally produced radium.

The Search for the New Element

The Curies found their pitchblende at a uranium mine in Czechoslovakia. The miners there took out the uranium, and dumped the rest. They were glad to be rid of it. Marie dissolved and heated bucketful after heavy bucketful, stirring the fuming liquids with an iron bar almost as big as herself. Day after day, month after month, what was left became smaller and smaller, purer and purer, and more radioactive. Although the work was desperately hard, it gave her a huge feeling of achievement. She and Pierre felt like explorers, charting land which no other human had seen.

But again, she had to prove it was really there. With what? The handful of pitchblende they had started with had almost run out. To extract any radium, they would need very large quantities of pitchblende. They also needed more room. They were offered an abandoned wooden shed just across the yard from the storeroom. It had a floor of beaten earth and a leaky glass roof. There were a few wooden tables and chairs, some gas burners and a rusty old stove. Unbearably hot in summer and freezing in winter, this is where Marie Curie, often completely exhausted, searched for radium.

Uranium is found naturally and is now an important mineral. Here a worker is laying explosives in a uranium mine in Mexico.

27

Finally, in March 1902, after four years' toil, Marie produced a tiny sample of a pure radium salt. It weighed one-tenth of a gramme – less than the weight of a potato crisp. But it was *a million times more radioactive* than uranium! And one night, while little Irène was sleeping, Marie and Pierre crept out of their house back to the shed. They stood there in the dark, 'stirred with new emotion and enchantment', gazing at the soft blue glow of the little tube on the shelf.

Helpers in the Curie's laboratory, working to separate radium from pitchblende.

Marie and Pierre with their speck of radium in a tube. This cartoon illustration is from a popular magazine of 1904.

Now at last, Marie could begin to prepare the thesis for her doctorate. In June, 1903, it was ready. Bronya persuaded Marie to buy a new dress for the occasion. She stood before the examiners, who questioned her closely. Scientists and friends watched. It was clear she knew more about this new subject – radioactivity – than anyone else in the room, even the examiners. They awarded Marie Curie the degree of Doctor of Science, 'with great distinction'. She was the first woman in Europe to receive such a degree.

Alfred Nobel, the Swedish chemist who invented dynamite. He made a fortune from his explosives and left it all in his will to a fund for prizes for literature, peace and the sciences.

But the greatest glory was still to come. In December that year, news came from Sweden that Marie and Pierre, together with Henri Becquerel who had first discovered the amazing rays, had been awarded the most important prize a scientist can win. Suddenly, they were famous around the world. Marie and Pierre Curie had won the Nobel Prize for Physics.

5 Fame Without Fortune

Although they were famous, the Curies were certainly not rich. They had already decided not to patent their discoveries. Why should they become very wealthy, when their knowledge, freely shared, could greatly benefit the whole world? However, this important decision committed them to living simply. Money was a constant problem. When Marie started her uranium research she had no income, and Pierre earned only a small salary as a lecturer at the Sorbonne. So Marie took a job too, teaching physics twice a week at a girls' school outside Paris.

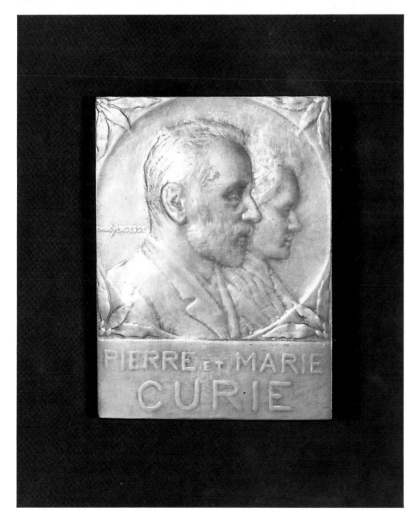

A commemorative medal of Marie and Pierre. It was struck to celebrate the Nobel prize which they received in 1903.

A photograph, taken in the early 1900s, of Marie at work in her laboratory.

Marie Curie was now a scientist, a teacher, a housewife and a mother. After feeding Irène in the mornings, she would go to the laboratory or take the slow tram to the girls' school. At home in the evening she would bathe the baby, feed her and play with her. Often she would read Irène a story, then put her to bed, sitting by her in the dark until she was asleep. Only then would she come downstairs to join her husband, to read, or perhaps to mend some clothes. But quite often, she went back to her laboratory for a few more hours.

The 'Miracle' Element

As Marie began to purify the radium, Pierre and other scientists began to study its properties. By the end of 1899, Pierre had found that radium produced three different kinds of rays, and that the rays made anything else near them radioactive. (In fact, the Curies' notebooks from this time are still so radioactive that they are dangerous to handle for very long.)

Scientists also investigated radium's powerful effect on the human body. Pierre soon discovered that radium could kill diseased cells in animals. It destroyed growths and tumours without harming healthy tissue. French doctors began treating human cancer patients with radium – sometimes with success. Radium was truly a miracle substance, a possible cure for cancer.

Here a patient is shown undergoing radiation treatment for cancer.

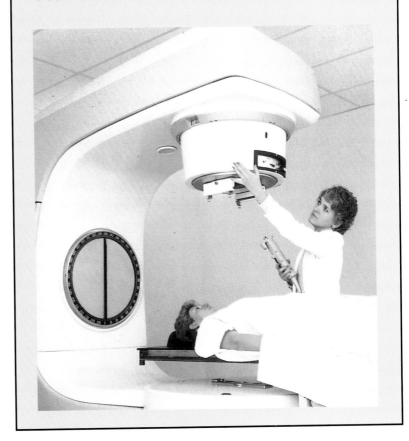

Throughout these years of stubborn hard work, Marie and Pierre suffered from nagging ill-health and continual tiredness. Pierre was often in great pain. Strangely, they never thought that their ill-health might be connected with their work. During the long hours that Marie and Pierre spent in their shed, they were breathing radioactive dust, and handling great quantities of radioactive ore. Other scientists often

High voltage equipment used by the Curies to test for radioactivity in their search for radium.

noticed that their fingers and hands were raw and red. By 1903, they were both suffering from what we would now call 'radiation sickness'.

When the Nobel Prize was announced, both Marie and Pierre felt too ill to travel to Stockholm to collect their award. They were distressed by Pierre's wracking bouts of rheumatism and fatigued by the hard work in terrible conditions, but they worked on at their teaching and their experiments with the radium. In the following year, 1904, Marie became pregnant again, and in December she gave birth to another girl, a sister for Irène, who they called Eve.

That year, too, the Sorbonne finally recognized the Curies' brilliance. Pierre was made a special professor, and Marie was appointed his Chief of Laboratory. Life gradually began to improve. The Curies could enjoy some Sunday afternoons in their garden, with a few scientific friends, chatting about the latest ideas and discoveries.

On 19 April 1906, after a few days of spring sunshine, it was pouring with rain. Pierre went round to see his publishers to talk over a manuscript, but their office was shut. He walked back, his eyes on the shiny slippery street, but his mind on something else. Absent-mindedly, he turned to cross the road, straight into the path of a heavy horse-drawn cart. The great back wheel crushed him. He died instantly.

Marie was devastated. Pierre had been the most important thing in her life. They had shared everything, even the work. She grieved for weeks. But gradually, she realized that she must carry on. She was only thirty-eight, and Irène and little Eve needed her. Marie was the only person in the world who could take over Pierre's work at the Sorbonne. So, in November, when the new university year began, she became the first woman ever to teach there. Two years later, the Sorbonne made her a Professor. Times were changing, and Marie Curie, with her indomitable will, was helping to change them.

6 Carrying on Alone

Marie in 1912. She continued her work after Pierre's death. Although exhausted and ill, she travelled to Sweden to receive her second Nobel prize shortly after this photograph was taken.

By now the children were growing up. Irène liked science, and she and her mother got on very well. Eve did not like science so much, but she was a cheerful addition to the serious Curie household, and loved music. She was a talented musician, and would one day be a concert pianist.

The university decided it would give Marie something that had always been denied to Pierre – a proper laboratory. It would be called 'The Institute of Radium', and would be built in the newly-named Rue Pierre Curie. Then, in 1911, another telegram arrived from Sweden. Marie Curie had been awarded a second Nobel prize. This time it was the Chemistry Prize, for her discovery of radium and polonium. It was the first time anyone had won two Nobel prizes.

Even though she was worn out, Marie determined that this time she would go to Sweden to collect her prize. But the journey exhausted her and she became extremely ill. She did not really recover until 1913, when she felt well enough to try a walking holiday in the mountains.

X-rays In Use

France was to suffer horribly during the years 1914–18, as millions of men were killed and injured in futile battles over a few hundred metres of muddy ground. Marie realized that with her knowledge she could help to save lives. She set up twenty mobile X-ray ambulances in borrowed cars, which the soldiers called 'little Curies', and two hundred more X-ray posts in hospitals near the battle front. She taught herself and Irène how to X-ray patients, and then began teaching others. It is estimated that during the war more than a million men were helped by Marie's X-ray stations.

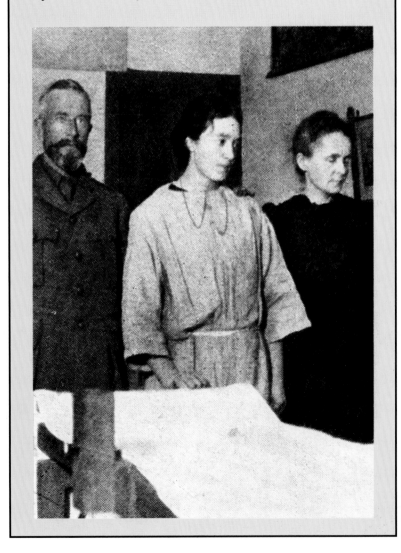

Marie at a British field hospital in 1914. She and Irène helped train people in the use of X-rays during the war.

Back in Paris, the Institute of Radium was nearly finished. It was to be in two sections. In one, Marie Curie was going to study radioactivity. In the other, a great professor of medicine, Dr Regaud, would carry out biological research into the medical effects of radium and its cancer-curing properties. The institute was opened on 31 July 1914. Four days later, the First World War began.

The war brought both X-rays and radiotherapy into full use in medicine for the first time. For two years after the war, at her Institute in Paris, Marie continued to train doctors and nurses in the use of X-rays. But there was still no money. The francs from the Nobel prizes had gone to help the French war effort. The Institute of Radium badly needed more of the enormously expensive radium, quite apart from more equipment and funds for research. Where was the money to come from?

The answer came, surprisingly, from a journalist. An American woman named Marie Maloney, who ran a magazine in New York, wrote to ask to see her 'for just a few minutes'. The two women became good friends straight away. Mrs Maloney promised that she could persuade the women of America to give enough money to pay for another gramme of radium. Within a year, she had done just that.

Mrs Maloney then asked Marie to come to the United States with her so that the President could give her the radium in person. Marie could hardly refuse, so in 1921, she sailed across the Atlantic with Irène and Eve. The trip was exciting and exhausting. Everyone wanted to see the woman who had given radium to the world. The tour took Marie from one side of the enormous country to the other. It was so successful that she was given enough money to buy a gramme of radium and still have 50,000 dollars left.

On 20 May, Marie went to the White House in Washington for the formal presentation. President Warren Harding handed over the single gramme of

The White House, where President Harding presented Marie Curie with a casket of radium to enable her to continue her research.

Working in her laboratory in Paris in 1917.

radium, in a mahogany box lined with lead to stop the radiation leaking out. The whole box weighed 50,000 grammes. The experience taught Marie that she could use her fame to raise badly-needed funds for research, and to draw people's attention to the importance of science.

Although Marie Curie made no big discoveries after Pierre's death in 1906, her work was still very important. Her teaching at the university, and at her Institute of Radium, inspired many young scientists. She travelled all over Europe, using her new skills in public relations to great effect. She made another trip to the United States in 1929, to raise money to buy radium for an Institute of Radium in her home city,

Warsaw. The Institute in Paris thrived, as Marie directed her brilliant team of scientists, including Irène, in the research into radioactivity. In the other half of the Institute, Dr Regaud studied the curative properties of radium, and its damaging effects.

For by now, people were beginning to realize that, as well as being a wonderful cure for cancer and other ailments, radium was very dangerous. We now know that radioactivity can cause cancer as well as cure it. It can also weaken the body's resistance to other infections and diseases. In the 1920s, though, these effects were not known.

A person receiving radiotherapy to treat a cancer. The illuminated discs indicate the areas which are to receive radiation.

One of the last photographs of Marie Curie, taken shortly before she died in 1934.

Marie Curie was extremely resilient. But eventually, the radium took its toll. Her body grew weaker, and she often felt dizzy and faint. One day in May 1934, she felt so ill that she left the Institute early. She quickly grew worse, and the doctors were puzzled. They diagnosed tuberculosis, and Marie was taken to a sanatorium in the south of France. In fact she was dying, of a blood disease called pernicious anaemia. It had been caused by handling radioactive substances, and breathing radioactive air, for so many years. In early July, Marie Curie died. She was buried two days later, in the same grave as Pierre.

7 Atoms and Radioactivity

There are now over one hundred known elements. Ninety-four of them occur naturally on Earth – the rest have been made in the laboratory. The elements are distinguished by the size and shape of their atoms, which give each its characteristic chemical properties – such as weight, density, melting-point or colour.

The atoms of any particular element are all the same as each other. Atoms of hydrogen, the simplest element, consist of a single proton, which is positively charged, and a single negative electron zipping around it. So it is electrically neutral – the single positive charge is balanced by the single negative charge.

The next heaviest element, helium, is more complicated. Its atom has two protons in its nucleus,

Irène Curie with her husband Frédéric Joliot. They won a Nobel prize in 1935 for their work on radioactivity.

balanced by two electrons outside. But it also has two neutral particles called 'neutrons' in its nucleus. So it weighs four times as much as a hydrogen atom, because of the two neutrons. (Electrons do not count – they weigh next to nothing in comparison.)

The Structure of the Atom

While Marie Curie was isolating radium from pitchblende, her husband Pierre and other scientists in France and England began to investigate the phenomenon which had led her to the new element: radioactivity. In doing so they unravelled the structure of the atom itself.

In 1897 Joseph Thomson discovered the existence of the electron. Then, in 1911, Ernest Rutherford, a New Zealand-born physicist, proposed the theory that atoms have a small nucleus containing protons surrounded by a cloud of electrons. James Chadwick, a British physicist working in Rutherford's laboratory, discovered the neutron in 1932. Two years later, Marie Curie's daughter, Irène, and her husband Frédéric Joliot discovered artificial radioactivity. Scientists were beginning to build up a clearer picture of how atoms are constructed and the nature of radioactivity.

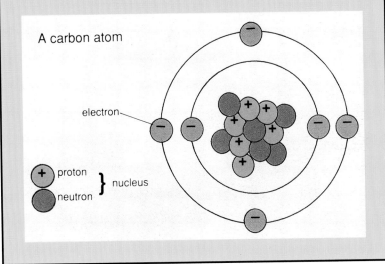

A carbon atom

electron

proton
neutron } nucleus

As the elements get heavier, so do their atoms. Element 6 is carbon. It has six protons and six neutrons in its nucleus, and six outer electrons. So it is twelve times as heavy as a hydrogen atom. A lead atom has eighty-two protons, (and therefore eighty-two electrons) – but in its nucleus, the protons are joined by 126 neutrons. That is why it is so heavy – 208 times the weight of a hydrogen atom.

Most atoms are stable, that is to say they do not change. But some – the radioactive ones – do. In a radioactive material, some of the atoms change into atoms of a *different element*. They break down of their own accord. They do this by spitting out some of the particles from their nuclei. This is radioactivity, and the particles thrown out are the radiation.

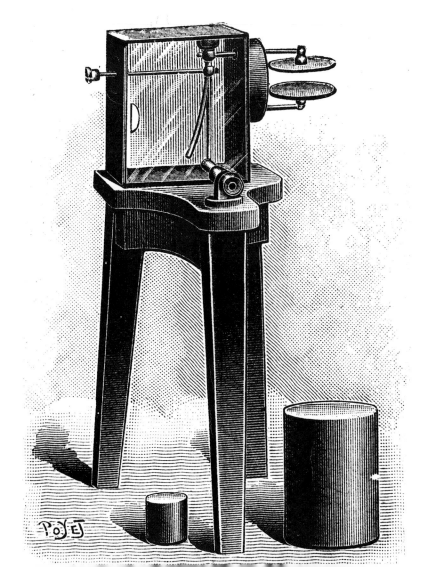

An electroscope used in the Curies' laboratory to detect the presence of radioactivity.

Atoms of any radioactive element break down at random – you cannot predict when any individual atom will do so. But some elements are more unstable than others. You can measure how long it takes for half the atoms of a block of a metal such as uranium$_{238}$ (so called because it is 238 times as heavy as hydrogen) to break down. This is its 'half-life', of 4,500 million years. If you start with a block of pure uranium$_{238}$ and wait all that time, half of it will have changed into something else. Another 4,500 million years later, a quarter of the uranium will still be left. The earth itself is only about 4,500 million years old, which is why there is plenty of uranium left on the planet.

But most radioactive elements are much less stable than uranium. Radium has a half life of 1,622 years. Radon has a half life of less than four days The half life of polonium is less than three minutes. Some break down in less than a second. The only reason these elements are found on earth today is that they are newly-formed all the time, as other elements break down.

The end product of all this breaking down is stable: it is familiar old lead. Lead is the end of the story, and one day very far from now, all the beautiful, gently glowing radium there is on earth, will have turned into that heavy, dull-looking metal.

A uranium deposit in Mexico.

Date Chart

1867 Marya Sklodowska, later Marie Curie, born in Warsaw.

1873 Marya's father removed from his job.

1878 Marya's mother dies of tuberculosis.

1882 Marya leaves school with a gold medal. She goes to stay with relatives in the country for a year.

1885 Bronya goes to Paris. Marya begins work as a governess.

1891 Marya enrols at the Sorbonne University.

1893 Marya (now Marie) comes first in her physics examination.

1894 Takes degree in mathematics. Meets Pierre Curie.

1895 Marie marries Pierre Curie.

1897 12 September, Irène, their first child is born.

1898 Pierre joins Marie in her search for radium.

1902 The Curies succeed in producing a speck of radium.

1903 Marie becomes the first European woman Doctor of Science. (December) Marie, Pierre and Henri Becquerel are awarded the Nobel Prize for Physics.

1904 6 December, Eve born.

1906 Pierre is killed in a road accident.

1911 Marie receives her second Nobel Prize, this time for chemistry.

1914 The Institute of Radium in Paris is completed.

1914 First World War breaks out. Marie organizes X-ray vans to help treat wounded soldiers and trains doctors and nurses in the use of X-rays.

1921 Marie sails to the USA with Irène and Eve. Receives a gramme of radium from President Harding at the White House.

1925 The Institute of Radium in Warsaw begun.

1929 Marie makes a second trip to the USA to raise money for radium for the Warsaw Institute.

1934 6 July, Marie Curie dies and is buried alongside husband Pierre.

Glossary

Atom The smallest unit into which any chemical element can be divided. Atoms consist of a very tiny nucleus surrounded by a cloud of electrons.

Biology The science which deals with all living organisms.

Chemical reaction The process, involving two or more substances, in which the compounds of elements split up and form new compounds.

Chemistry The science which deals with how substances are made up and how they act under different conditions.

Electron A very light part of an atom with a negative electric charge.

Electroscope An instrument used for detecting and measuring electricity.

Element A substance which cannot be 'decomposed' or split up into a simpler form.

Mineral A natural substance obtained from the earth by mining.

Neutron A tiny part of an atom without an electric charge.

Nucleus The central part of something about which other parts are grouped.

Ore Rock or mineral from which metal can be obtained.

Physics The science which deals with the study of the Universe, matter, energy, heat, light, electricity, magetism and sound.

Pitchblende A soft rock which contains uranium and radium.

Proton A very tiny part of an atom with a positive electric charge.

Radioactive Having the property of giving off radiation.

Radiotherapy The treatment of disease using X-rays or other forms of radiation.

Radon Radioactive gas which comes from the disintegration of radium.

X-ray A penetrating form of radiation that can pass through something solid.

Books to read

Madam Curie (History Makers) by Jacqueline Henrie (Chambers, 1977)

Marie Curie by Robert Reid (Collins, 1974)

Marie Curie by Angela Bull (H. Hamilton, 1986)

Marie Curie by Edwina Conner (Wayland, 1987)

Marie Curie and the Discovery of Radium by Ann E. Steinke (Barron, 1988)

Marie Curie the Polish Scientist who Discovered Radium by Beverley Birch (Exley, 1988)

Picture acknowledgements

Marie Curie Cancer Care iii, 7, 8, 14, 18, 38; Mary Evans cover, 25, 29, 30; Billie Love 9, 10, 13, 16, 17, 20, 29; The Mansell Collection 15; Popperfoto 23, 32, 37, 41, 43; Ann Ronan Picture Library 17 (bottom), 19, 22, 26, 28, 31, 34, 36, 44; Science Photo Library 21, 26; Science Photo Library/Tim Beddow 4, /Martin Dohrn 40, /Stevie Grand 33, /David Leah27, 45, /US Department of Energy 6; Wayland/UKAE 5. Diagram of page 43 by Jenny Hughes. Cover illustration by Gill Andrae-Reid.

Index